A Teenager's Illustrated Guide to the Early Church Fathers

A Teenager's Illustrated Guide to the Early Church Fathers

A.M. Overett

A Teenager's Illustrated Guide to the Early Church Fathers

© A.M. Overett 2024

Published by
Lighthouse Christian Publishing
SAN 257-4330
228 Freedom Parkway
Hoschton, GA 30548
United States of America

www.lighthousechristianpublishing.com

Table of Contents:

Introduction:

Welcome to the **Teenager's Illustrated Guide to the Early Church Fathers**!
We hope you enjoy this wonderful journey through the lives of the great men (and women) of the early Church.

In this book, you will learn about the great pillars of the church, who took the teachings of Jesus and the Apostles then expounded upon them and showed us how we can apply these great truths to our lives.

Many Christians today believe that we can pick up the Bible, start reading it, and immediately understand its meaning. While to some extent that might be true, we can get even greater insights from the men who first viewed, compiled and interpreted the sacred book's contents. Through these inspired men, we learn what the role of the church is, how the church is to be administered, and how we should live our daily lives. It was these men who brought us the concepts that are not found in the Bible, defining such ideas as predestination, transubstantiation, the Holy Trinity, and much more.

This book typically devotes a page to each Church Father with a short biography as well as a list of some of their key writings and how we can apply them to our own lives.

Along with information about the Church Fathers, we also give descriptions of the world they were living in, how the Church was functioning at the time, and what obstacles they faced when spreading and preaching the Gospel.

And finally, not to ignore our sisters in faith, there is a section devoted to some of the female saints and theologians who contributed greatly to the growth of the Church.

The Church Fathers are presented in chronological order and this is not a complete list of all those people in that category but covers most of the main and more influential theologians and Christian thinkers. With future editions, we hope to add more of the Fathers regularly.

Saint Ignatius: (circa 35 - 108 A.D.)

Ignatius of Antioch was a first-century Christian writer. While traveling to Rome, Ignatius wrote letters or "epistles" to the Early Christian communities. These became part of a collection of works by the Apostolic Fathers. "Apostolic Fathers," were the Early Church Fathers who had known or were heavily influenced by the original Twelve Apostles. He is considered one of the three most important, with Clement of Rome and Polycarp. These letters featured early Christian theology and addressed important ideas like ecclesiology (the role of the church and its governance), the sacraments, and the role of bishops.

Little is known of Ignatius' life apart from his epistles and later church traditions and teachings. Ignatius converted to Christianity at an early age and tradition identifies him and his friend Polycarp as disciples of John the Apostle.

Ignatius was eventually chosen to serve as Bishop of Antioch. Theodoret of Cyrrhus claimed that St. Peter directed that Ignatius be appointed bishop. Ignatius was called *Theophorous* (God-Bearer). Tradition states that he was one of the children whom Jesus Christ took in his arms and blessed.

Writings:

The Epistles of St. Ignatius.

What are some insights that we can get from St. Ignatius writings?

In his epistle to the Ephesians, Ignatius writes this about the Lord's advent...

Now the virginity of Mary was hidden from the prince of this world, as was also her offspring, and the death of the Lord; three mysteries of renown, which were wrought in silence, but have been revealed to us. A star shone forth in heaven above all that were before it, and its light was inexpressible, while its novelty struck men with astonishment. And all the rest of the stars, with the sun and moon, formed a chorus to this star. It far exceeded them all in brightness, and agitation was felt as to whence this new spectacle [proceeded]. Hence worldly wisdom became folly; conjuration was seen to be mere trifling; and magic became utterly ridiculous. Every law of wickedness vanished away; the darkness of ignorance was dispersed; and tyrannical authority was destroyed, God being manifested as a man, and man displaying power as God. But neither was the former a mere imagination, nor did the second imply a bare humanity; but the one was absolutely true, and the other an economical arrangement. Now that received a beginning which was perfected by God. Henceforth all things were in a state of tumult, because He meditated the abolition of death.

Clement of Rome: (35 to circa 99 A.D.)

Clement of Rome also known as **Pope Clement I**, was the bishop of Rome in the late first century A.D. He is noted by Irenaeus and Tertullian as the Bishop of Rome, from 88 A.D. to his death in 99 A.D. He has been called the first Apostolic Father of the Church, one of the three chief ones together with Polycarp and Ignatius of Antioch. These three were closely associated with the original Twelve Apostles of Jesus.

Few details are known about Clement's life. Clement was said to have been consecrated by St. Peter, and he is known to have been a leading member of the Church in Rome in the late first century. Early church lists place him as the second or third Bishop of Rome. The Catholic Church lists him as the fourth pope. It was said that Clement died in Greece in the third year of Emperor Trajan's reign, or 101 AD.

There is a 4th-century legend that while in exile, Clement, while looking for water for all the workers, saw a lamb on a hill. He went to where that lamb was standing and hit the ground with his pickax causing water to flow out of the hill.

Writings:

The First Epistle of Clement to the Corinthians.

What can we learn and apply from Clement of Rome?

These things, beloved, we write unto you, not merely to admonish you of your duty, but also to remind ourselves. For we are struggling on the same arena, and the same conflict is assigned to both of us. Wherefore let us give up vain and fruitless cares, and approach to the glorious and venerable rule of our holy calling. Let us attend to what is good, pleasing, and acceptable in the sight of Him who formed us. Let us look steadfastly to the blood of Christ, and see how precious that blood is to God, which, having been shed for our salvation, has set the grace of repentance before the whole world.

Polycarp: (69 to 156 A.D.)

Polycarp was a Christian Bishop of Smyrna, the city today known as Izmir in Turkey. According to the Martyrdom of Polycarp, he died being bound and burned at the stake, then stabbed when the fire failed to consume his body. Polycarp is regarded as a saint and Church Father in most Christian denominations.

Both Irenaeus and Tertullian say that Polycarp had been a disciple of John the Apostle. St. Jerome writes that Polycarp was a disciple of John the Apostle and that John had ordained him as a Bishop of Smyrna. Polycarp is regarded as one of the three chief Apostolic Fathers, along with Clement of Rome and Ignatius of Antioch.

Writings:

The Epistle of Polycarp to the Philippians.

What are some of Polycarp's writings that we can apply to our own lives?

Stand fast, therefore, in these things, and follow the example of the Lord, being firm and unchangeable in the faith, loving the brotherhood, and being attached to one another, joined together in the truth, exhibiting the meekness of the Lord in your intercourse with one another, and despising no one. When you can do good, defer it not, because "alms delivers from death." Be all of you subject one to another "having your conduct blameless among the Gentiles," that ye may both receive praise for your good works, and the Lord may not be blasphemed through you. But woe to him by whom the name of the Lord is blasphemed![60] Teach, therefore, sobriety to all, and manifest it also in your own conduct.

What was the first century like for the Christian Church?

In the first century, as the Church was just beginning, most of the known world was under Roman control. The Romans were one of the most advanced cultures at the time, with many technological wonders. The Romans created aqueducts that brought water to the various villages and towns within the Roman Empire. What was previously a laborious task of bringing water daily from a well or other water source, was revolutionized by the aqueduct. For some noblemen and politicians, the water was "pipped" right into their homes. It was an early forerunner of household plumbing.

Another great triumph of the Romans was their vast network of roads. Throughout their empire, they constructed a system of highways that were often made of stone or brick so as not to be impacted by rain and the elements thus avoiding the slowdown of transportation.

Along with their great bridges and other architecture, the Romans were an advanced civilization for their time.

The network of roads created by the Romans allowed for the easy movement of their great armies. The flow of men, materials, and weapons allowed them to expand their empire. They were soon in control of much of the Western world of the time.

One of the ways in which the Romans helped keep the peoples of their conquered territories under subjugation was with the use of terror; beatings, flogging, and many violent forms of the death penalty. Many Christians, deemed as a threat to their mythology, were used as bait for horrible Roman games of torture and were thrown into arenas with wild animals.

And of course one of their most popular deterrents was crucifixion. This was a humiliating and extremely painful form of the death penalty. And as we of course know this is how our Lord suffered. All because of our sins. As this message of hope and redemption was spread by the Apostles and early followers like the Church Fathers, because of immense persecution the Christian communities were soon driven "underground" and were meeting in secret in homes, caves, or any structure that would not draw attention to themselves.

Justin Martyr: (100 to 165 A.D.)

Justin Martyr also known as **Justin the Philosopher** was an early apologist of the Christian faith.

Most of his writings did not survive antiquity. *The First Apology* defends Christian morality/living as well as provides various arguments to convince the Roman emperor to abandon his persecution of the Church.

Having grown up in Greece, he was well acquainted with Greek philosophy, and having been a student of Stoicism and Platonism. His studies in Greek philosophy, especially of Plato, influenced his beliefs.

Justin was martyred, along with some of his students, and is venerated as a saint by the Catholic Church and many other Christian denominations.

What is an apologist? Is it someone who says, "I am sorry" a lot? Here's a definition – An apologist is the religious discipline of defending religious doctrines through systematic argumentation and discourse.

> **Writings:**
>
> The First Apology, The Second Apology, The Dialogue of Justin Martyr and Trypho.
>
> **How can we apply to our own lives what Justin taught?**

But we have received by tradition that God does not need the material offerings which men can give, seeing, indeed, that He Himself is the provider of all things. And we have been taught, and are convinced, and do believe, that He accepts those only who imitate the excellences which reside in Him, temperance, and justice, and philanthropy, and as many virtues as are peculiar to a God who is called by no proper name. And we have been taught that He in the beginning did of His goodness, for man's sake, create all things out of unformed matter; and if men by their works show themselves worthy of this His design, they are deemed worthy, and so we have received—of reigning in company with Him, being delivered from corruption and suffering. For as in the beginning He created us when we were not, so do we consider that, in like manner, those who choose what is pleasing to Him are, on account of their choice, deemed worthy of incorruption and of fellowship with Him.

St. Irenaeus: (130 to 202 A.D.)

Irenaeus was a Greek bishop known for his spreading of the gospel throughout southern France and other areas of southern Europe. He was also known for his work in theology whereby was an opponent of the growing Gnostic heresy. It was said that he had seen and heard the preaching of Polycarp, who in turn was said to have heard John the Evangelist, and thus was the last-known living connection with the Apostles.

In opposing the gnostic sects, who were claiming a secret wisdom, he offered three pillars of orthodoxy; the scriptures, the tradition handed down from the apostles, and the teaching of the apostles' successors.

Irenaeus is the earliest of the Church Fathers to regard all four of the now canonical gospels as essential. He is recognized as a saint in the Catholic and the Eastern Orthodox Churches. Pope Francis declared Irenaeus the 37th Doctor of the Church on 21 January 2022.

What is a "Doctor" of the Church? Can they dispense medical advice to parishioners? No, a Doctor of the Church is a title given by the Catholic Church to saints recognized as having made a significant contribution to theology or doctrine through research, study, or writing.

Writings:

Against Heresies

What can we learn from Irenaeus' writings?

The Church, though dispersed through our the whole world, even to the ends of the earth, has received from the apostles and their disciples this faith: [She believes] in one God, the Father Almighty, Maker of heaven, and earth, and the sea, and all things that are in them; and in one Christ Jesus, the Son of God, who became incarnate for our salvation; and in the Holy Spirit, who proclaimed through the prophets the dispensations of God, and the advents, and the birth from a virgin, and the passion, and the resurrection from the dead, and the ascension into heaven in the flesh of the beloved Christ Jesus, our Lord, and His [future] manifestation from heaven in the glory of the Father "to gather all things in one," and to raise up anew all flesh of the whole human race, in order that to Christ Jesus, our Lord, and God, and Savior, and King, according to the will of the invisible Father, "every knee should bow, of things in heaven, and things in earth, and things under the earth, and that every tongue should confess" to Him, and that He should execute just judgment towards all; that He may send "spiritual wickednesses," and the angels who transgressed and became apostates, together with the ungodly, and unrighteous, and wicked, and profane among men, into everlasting fire; but may, in the exercise of His grace, confer immortality on the righteous, and holy, and those who have kept His commandments, and have persevered in His love, some from the beginning [of their Christian course], and others from [the date of] their repentance, and may surround them with everlasting glory.

Clement of Alexandria: (150 TO 215 A.D.)

Titus Flavius Clemens, also known as **Clement of Alexandria**, was a theologian and philosopher who taught at the *Catechetical School of Alexandria*. Origen and Alexander of Jerusalem were at one time his students. A convert to Christianity, he was an educated man who was familiar with Greek philosophy and literature. Like Justin Martyr, Clement was influenced by Hellenistic philosophy to a great extent, and in particular, by Plato and the Stoics. His secret works, which exist only in fragments, suggest that he was familiar with pre-Christian Jewish esotericism and Gnosticism as well.

Writings:

Exhortation to the Heathen, the Stromata, The Fragments, The Instructor, Salvation of the Rich Man.

How can we apply what Clement of Alexandria taught?

Speaking of the Advent of Jesus…

He that is truly most manifest Deity, He that is made equal to the Lord of the universe; because He was His Son, and the Word was in God, not disbelieved in by all when He was first preached, nor altogether unknown when, assuming the character of man, and fashioning Himself in flesh, He enacted the drama of human salvation: for He was a true champion and a fellow-champion with the creature. And being communicated most speedily to men, having dawned from His Father's counsel quicker than the sun, with the most perfect ease He made God shine on us. Whence He was and what He was, He showed by what He taught and exhibited, manifesting Himself as the Herald of the Covenant, the Reconciler, our Savior, the Word, the Fount of life, the Giver of peace, diffused over the whole face of the earth; by whom, so to speak, the universe has already become an ocean of blessings.

Alexandria:

Why was the port city of Alexandria important to the early Christian Church?

Alexandria was an important port city not only from the standpoint of trade and the gateway to the Nile, but the city itself was an architectural marvel of its time. Founded by Alexander the Great in 331 B.C., the city became a center for Hellenic scholarship and science. With its great library, it was a hub for all things intellectual.

It was here that Christian scholarship flourished with the founding of The **Catechetical School of Alexandria.** Some of the great early Church Fathers were educated or taught at the school including Clement of Alexandria, Athenagoras, and Origen. Saints Jerome and Basil also visited the school to interact with its scholars.

The port's lighthouse was also considered a technological marvel and was one of the **Seven Wonders of the Ancient World.**

Tertullian: (155 to 240 A.D.)

Tertullian was an early Christian writer from Carthage in what is today the country of Tunisia. He was the first Christian author to create an extensive body of theological works in Latin. He was an apologist and was opposed to various heresies at the time, including Christian Gnosticism. Tertullian has been called "the father of Latin Christianity as well as "the founder of Western theology".

Tertullian conceived new theological ideas and helped advance early Church doctrines. He is perhaps most famous for being the first writer in Latin known to use the term **trinity**. Later he had issues with the Church with some of his teachings. He believed in the subordination of the Son and Spirit to the Father, which was later rejected by the Church. He later left the Church and joined the Montanist sect.

Writings:

Ad Martyras and the Holy Passion of the Martyrs Perpetua and Felicitas, Against the Valentinians, The Five Books Against Marcion, Exhortation to Modesty, On Prayer, On Baptism, On the Resurrection of the Flesh.

How can we apply what Tertullian taught?

Tertullian's thoughts on the Roman Empire…

. There is also another and a greater necessity for our offering prayer on behalf of the emperors, nay, for the complete stability of the empire, and for Roman interests in general. For we know that a mighty shock impending over the whole earth—in fact, the very end of all things threatening dreadful woes—is only retarded by the continued existence of the Roman empire. We have no desire, then, to be overtaken by these dire events; and in praying that their coming may be delayed, we are lending our aid to Rome's duration.

Origen: (184 to 253 A.D.)

Origen of Alexandria also known as **Origen Adamantius**, was an early Christian scholar, and theologian who was born and began his career in Alexandria. He was a prolific writer who wrote roughly 2,000 treatises on multiple theological topics. He was one of the most influential figures in early Christian theology and apologetics and was described as "the greatest genius the early church ever produced".

His mother prevented Origen from being taken by the authorities which would have ultimately led to his martyrdom. At eighteen years of age, he became a catechist at the **Catechetical School of Alexandra**. During this time he was devoted to his studies, leading the lifestyle of an ascetic.

Origen came into conflict with Demetrius, the bishop of Alexandria, in 231 after he was ordained as a presbyter by his friend Theoclistus, the bishop of Caesarea, while on a journey to Athens through Palestine. Origen founded the **Christian School of Caesarea**, where he taught many subjects and became regarded by the churches of Palestine and Arabia as the ultimate authority on all matters of theology. He was tortured during the Decian Persecution in 250 and died three to four years later from his injuries.

Writings:

De Principiis, Origen Against Celsus, A Letter from Origen to Africanus

How can we apply what Origen taught?

"At the end and consummation of the world, when souls and rational creatures shall have been sent forth as from bolts and barriers, some of them walk slowly on account of their slothful habits, others fly with rapid flight on account of their diligence. And since all are possessed of free will, and may of their own accord admit either of good or evil, the former will be in a worse condition than they are at present, while the latter will advance to a better state of things; because different conduct and varying wills will admit of a different condition in either direction, i.e., angels may become men or demons, and again from the latter they may rise to be men or angels."

St. Cyprian: (210 to 258 A.D.)

Cyprian was the Bishop of Carthage and an early Christian author, many of whose Latin works are still in existence. He is recognized as a saint in the Western and Eastern churches.

St. Cyprian was born toward the beginning of the 3rd century in what is today the country of Tunisia in North Africa. After converting to Christianity, he later became a bishop in 249. A controversial figure, he had strong views on pastoral care and opposition to the Novatian heresy. The outbreak of the **Plague of Cyprian** (named after him due to his writings of it), and eventual martyrdom at Carthage, established his sanctity in the eyes of the Church.

His skillful Latin rhetoric led to his being considered the pre-eminent Latin writer of Western Christianity until Jerome and Augustine.

Writings:

The Epistles of St. Cyprian, The Treatises of St. Cyprian

How can we apply what St. Cyprian taught?

Let us only, without ceasing to ask, and with full faith that we shall receive, in simplicity and unanimity beseech the Lord, entreating not only with groaning but with tears, as it behooves those to entreat who are situated between the ruins of those who wail, and the remnants of those who fear; between the manifold slaughter of the yielding, and the little firmness of those who still stand. Let us ask that peace may be soon restored; that we may be quickly helped in our concealments and our dangers; that those things may be fulfilled which the Lord deigns to show to his servants,—the restoration of the Church, the security of our salvation; after the rains, serenity; after the darkness, light; after the storms and whirlwinds, a peaceful calm; the affectionate aids of paternal love, the accustomed grandeurs of the divine majesty whereby both the blasphemy of persecutors may be restrained, the repentance of the lapsed renewed, and the steadfast faith of the persevering may glory. I bid you, beloved brethren, ever heartily farewell; and have me in remembrance. Salute the brotherhood in my name; and remind them to remember me. Farewell.

Carthage:

On the northern coast of what is today Tunisia, lay the great city-state of Carthage. Carthage was home to two of the great early church fathers; Tertullian and St. Cyprian. For many centuries, the Carthaginian people were a strong force and contested the Romans as one of the supreme powers of the Mediterranean. They, like the Romans, were an ingenious people, creating an impressive port and constructing fine sailing vessels that would set sail from that port.

Eventually, they came under Roman rule and during that period several key Christian scholars emerged from the great city. The city though will be forever remembered as a great power and for the great ships that sailed from it.

Archelaus: (? to 258 A.D.)

Archelaus was the Bishop of Carrhae. Carrhae was the ancient name for the city in Turkey which today is known as Harran. In 278 A.D., he held a public dispute with several Manichaeans - an account of which he published in Syriac. The work was soon translated both into Greek and into Latin. ***The Acts of Disputation of Archelaus, bishop of Cashar in Mesopotamia.*** For some time, the *Acts* served as an essential source for Mani's life and Manichaeism.

Catholic Culture website writes this of Manichaeism…

A dualistic heresy initiated in the third century by a Persian named Mani, Manes, or Manichaeus (215-75). He was considered divinely inspired, and he gained a large following. In the Manichaean system there are two ultimate sources of creation, the one good and the other evil. God is the creator of all that is good, and Satan of all that is evil. Man's spirit is from God, his body is from the devil. There is a constant struggle between the forces of good and those of evil. Good triumphs over evil only insofar as the spirit rises superior to the body. In practice Manichaeism denies human responsibility for the evil that one does, on the premise that this is not due to one's own free will but to the dominance of Satan's power in one's life.

Writings:

The Acts of Disputation of Archelaus with the Heresiarch Manes

How can we apply what Archelaus taught?

Archelaus speaking on Manichaeism…

He holds also that God has no part with the world itself, and finds no pleasure in it, by reason of its having been made a spoil of from the first by the princes, and on account of the ill that rose on it. Wherefore He sends and takes away from them day by day the soul belonging to Him, through the medium of these luminaries, the sun and the moon, by which the whole world and all creation are dominated.

Alexander 1 of Alexandria: (? to 326-328 A.D.)

Alexander I of Alexandria was the 19th Pope and Patriarch of Alexandria. During his time, he dealt with major issues facing the Church. These included the dating of Easter, the actions of Meletus of Lycopolis, and a greater issue, **Arianism**. He was the leader of the opposition to Arianism at the **First Council of Nicaea**. He also mentored St. Athanasius who would become one of the Church Fathers.

Little is known about Alexander's early years. During his time as a priest, he experienced the bloody persecutions of Christians by the Roman Emperors before Constantine.

One of the main controversies Alexander faced was a schismatic sect, led by Erescentius. This was the dispute involving the timing of Easter. Alexander ended up writing a special treatise on the controversy, in which he cited earlier statements regarding the matter by **Dionysius of Alexandria**. Alexander's efforts, while they did serve to quiet the dispute, were not enough to eliminate the controversies, although the First Council of Nicaea, held during his tenure, did resolve the matter.

Writings:

Epistles on the Arian Heresy And the Deposition of Arius.

How can we apply what Alexander taught?

Alexander discussing the heresy of Arianism…

For since they call in question all pious and apostolical doctrine, after the manner of the Jews, they have constructed a workshop for contending against Christ, denying the Godhead of our Savior, and preaching that He is only the equal of all others. And having collected all the passages which speak of His plan of salvation and His humiliation for our sakes, they endeavor from these to collect the preaching of their impiety, ignoring altogether the passages in which His eternal Godhead and unutterable glory with the Father is set forth.

St. Athanasius: (296-298 to 373 A.D.)

Athanasius I of Alexandria also called **Athanasius the Great**, **Athanasius the Confessor**, was a theologian and the 20th patriarch of Alexandria (as **Athanasius I**). His intermittent episcopacy spanned 45 years (c. 8 June 328 – 2 May 373), of which over 17 encompassed five exiles, when he was replaced on the order of four different Roman emperors. Athanasius was a chief proponent of **Trinitarianism** against Arianism.

Conflict with Arius, as well as with Roman emperors, impacted Athanasius' career. In 325, Athanasius began his leading role against the Arians as a deacon and assistant to Bishop Alexander of Alexandria during the First Council of Nicaea. Roman Emperor Constantine the Great had convened the council in May–August 325 to address the Arian position that the Son of God, Jesus of Nazareth, is of a distinct substance from the Father.

Within a few years of Athanasius' death, Gregory of Nazianzus called him the "Pillar of the Church". His writings were well regarded by subsequent Church Fathers, who noted their devotion to the **Word-become-man**, pastoral concern, and interest in monasticism. Athanasius is one of the **Four Great Eastern Doctors** of the Church in the Catholic Church. Some argue Athanasius was the first person to list the 27 books of the New Testament canon that are in use today.

Writings:
The Incarnation of the Word

How can we apply what St. Athanasius taught?

In regard to the making of the universe and the creation of all things there have been various opinions, and each person has propounded the theory that suited his own taste. For instance, some say that all things are self-originated and, so to speak, haphazard. The Epicureans are among these; they deny that there is any Mind behind the universe at all. This view is contrary to all the facts of experience, their own existence included. For if all things had come into being in this automatic fashion, instead of being the outcome of Mind, though they existed, they would all be uniform and without distinction. In the universe everything would be sun or moon or whatever it was, and in the human body the whole would be hand or eye or foot. But in point of fact the sun and the moon and the earth are all different things, and even within the human body there are different members, such as foot and hand and head. This distinctness of things argues not a spontaneous generation but a prevenient Cause; and from that Cause we can apprehend God, the Designer and Maker of all.

The First Council of Nicaea: (325 A.D.)

The **First Council of Nicaea** was a council of Christian bishops convened in the city of Nicaea (now Iznik, Turkey) by the Roman Emperor Constantine 1. The Council of Nicaea met from May to the end of July 325.

The First Council of Nicaea was the first time that an attempt was made to summon a general council of the whole church in every part of the Roman Empire. Much was accomplished especially concerning the divine nature of God the Son and his relationship to God the Father, the construction of the first part of the Nicene Creed (See below), mandating uniform observance of the date of Easter, and the promulgation of early canon law. For the first time, the technical aspects of Christology were discussed. Through it, a precedent was set for subsequent general councils to adopt creeds and canons. This Council is generally considered the beginning of the period of the first seven ecumenical councils in the history of Christianity.

Constantine had invited all 1,800 bishops of the Christian church within the Roman Empire (about 1,000 in the East and 800 in the West), but a smaller and unknown number attended.

We believe in one God, the Father Almighty, the maker of heaven and earth, of things visible and invisible. And in one Lord Jesus Christ, the Son of God, the begotten of God the Father, the Only-begotten, that is of the substance of the Father. God of God, Light of Light, true God of true God, begotten and not made; of the very same nature of the Father, by Whom all things came into being, in heaven and on earth, visible and invisible. Who for us humanity and for our salvation came down from heaven, was incarnate, became human, was born perfectly of the holy virgin Mary by the Holy Spirit. By whom He took body, soul, and mind, and everything that is in man, truly and not in semblance. He suffered, was crucified, was buried, rose again on the third day, ascended into heaven with the same body, [and] sat at the right hand of the Father. He is to come with the same body and with the glory of the Father, to judge the living and the dead; of His kingdom, there is no end. We believe in the Holy Spirit, the uncreate and the perfect; Who spoke through the Law, the prophets, and the Gospels; Who came down upon the Jordan, preached through the apostles, and lived in the saints. We believe also in only One, Universal, Apostolic, and [Holy] Church; in one baptism with repentance for the remission and forgiveness of sins; and in the resurrection of the dead, in the everlasting judgment of souls and bodies, in the Kingdom of Heaven and in the everlasting life.

St. Basil the Great: (330 - 378 A.D.)

Basil of Caesarea, also called **Saint Basil the Great** was a bishop of Caesarea Mazaca in Cappadocia, Eastern Turkey. A theologian and major supporter of the Nicene Creed who also opposed the heresies of Arianism and the followers of Apollinaris of Laodicea. His abilities as a theologian and his influence within the Church made Basil a powerful advocate regarding the Nicene position.

St. Basil was also known for service to the poor. He established guidelines for monastic life which focus on community life, liturgical prayer, and manual labor. He is considered a saint by the traditions of both Eastern and Western Christianity.

Basil, together with his brother Gregory of Nyssa and his friend Gregory of Nazianzus, are collectively known as the Cappadocian Fathers. The Eastern Orthodox and Eastern Catholic Church have given him the title of Great Hierarch. He is recognized as a Doctor of the Church in the Roman Catholic Church. He is sometimes referred to by the epithet "revealer of heavenly mysteries".

Writings:

De Spiritu Sancto, Hexeameron.

How can we apply what St. Basil taught?

Our opponents, while they thus artfully and perversely encounter our argument, cannot even have recourse to the plea of ignorance. It is obvious that they are annoyed with us for completing the doxology to the Only Begotten together with the Father, and for not separating the Holy Spirit from the Son. On this account they style us innovators, revolutionizers, phrase-coiners, and every other possible name of insult. But so far am I from being irritated at their abuse, that, were it not for the fact that their loss causes me "heaviness and continual sorrow," I could almost have said that I was grateful to them for the blasphemy, as though they were agents for providing me with blessing. For "blessed are ye," it is said, "when men shall revile you for my sake.

St. Ambrose: (340 - 397 A.D.)

Ambrose of Milan venerated as **Saint Ambrose**, was a theologian and statesman who served as Bishop of Milan from 374 to 397. As a great theologian, he fiercely promoted Roman Christianity against Arianism and paganism. He had extensive writings, with *De officiis ministrorum* (377–391), and the exegetical *Exameron* (386–390) being some of his best-known. He possessed musical ability and was also a hymnographer.

While serving as the Roman governor of Aemilia-Liguria in Milan, Ambrose was unexpectedly made Bishop of Milan in 374. It was thought that Ambrose created an antiphonal chant, known as the **Ambrosian Chant**, and composed the "Te Deum" hymn. Composition of at least four hymns, including the well-known "Veni redemptory gentium", has been attributed to him. He also had a notable influence on St. Augustine, whom he helped convert to Christianity.

Western Christianity identified Ambrose as one of its four traditional Doctors of the Church. He is considered a saint by the Catholic Church, Eastern Orthodox Church, the Anglican Church, and various other protestant denominations, and venerated as the patron saint of Milan and beekeepers.

Writings:

Exposition of the Christian Faith, On the Duties of the Clergy, On Repentance, On the Holy Spirit.

How can we apply what St. Ambrose taught?

This is mentioned as the only cause which will mitigate the wrath of God against their sin, if they honor the widow, and execute true judgment for minors, for thus we read: "Judge the fatherless, deal justly with the widow, and come let us reason together, saith the Lord." And elsewhere: "The Lord shall maintain the orphan and the widow." And again: "I will abundantly bless her widow." Wherein also the likeness of the Church is foreshadowed. You see, then, holy widows, that that office which is honored by the assistance of divine grace must not be degraded by impure desire.

St. Jerome: (342 - 420 A.D.)

Jerome also known as **Jerome of Stridon**, was an early Christian priest, confessor, theologian, translator, and historian; he is commonly known as **Saint Jerome**.

Jerome was commissioned by the pope to translate the Bible into Latin, which became known as the "Vulgate." Jerome attempted to create a translation of the Old Testament based on a Hebrew version, rather than the Greek Septuagint. In addition to his biblical works, he wrote various theological essays.

Jerome was known for his teachings on Christian morality. Many of his teachings focused on the lives of women, showing them how to devote their lives to God. This was influenced by his close relationship with several prominent women who were members of affluent senatorial families.

Due to his work, Jerome is recognized as a saint and Doctor of the Church by the Roman Catholic Church. His feast day is 30 September.

Writings:

Jerome's Apology against Rufinus, Lives of Illustrious Men.

How can we apply what St. Jerome taught?

Simon Peter the son of John, from the village of Bethsaida in the province of Galilee, brother of Andrew the apostle, and himself chief of the apostles, after having been bishop of the church of Antioch and having preached to the Dispersion—the believers in circumcision, in Pontus, Galatia, Cappadocia, Asia and Bithynia—pushed on to Rome in the second year of Claudius to overthrow Simon Magus, and held the sacerdotal chair there for twenty-five years until the last, that is the fourteenth, year of Nero. At his hands he received the crown of martyrdom being nailed to the cross with his head towards the ground and his feet raised on high, asserting that he was unworthy to be crucified in the same manner as his Lord. He wrote two epistles which are called Catholic, the second of which, on account of its difference from the first in style, is considered by many not to be by him. Then too the Gospel according to Mark, who was his disciple and interpreter, is ascribed to him. On the other hand, the books, of which one is entitled his Acts, another his Gospel, a third his Preaching, a fourth his Revelation, a fifth his "Judgment" are rejected as apocryphal. Buried at Rome in the Vatican near the Triumphal Way he is venerated by the whole world.

St. John Chrysostom: (347 - 407 A.D.)

John Chrysostom was an important early Christian leader who served as archbishop of Constantinople. He is known for his excellent public speaking, his condemnation of abuse of authority by both church and civic leaders, his *Divine Liturgy of Saint John Chrysostom*, and his ascetic sensibilities. The name (*Chrysostomos*, anglicized as Chrysostom) translates as "golden-mouthed," an acknowledgment of his great eloquence. Chrysostom was among the most prolific authors in the early Christian Church.

He is honored as a saint and as a Doctor of the Church in the Roman Catholic Church as well as other denominations. Because the date of his death is occupied by the feast of the Exaltation of the Holy Cross (14 September), the General Roman Calendar celebrates him since 1970 on the previous day, 13 September; from the 13th century to 1969 it did so on 27 January, the anniversary of the translation of his body to Constantinople.

Writings:

Treatise Concerning the Priesthood.

How can we apply what St. Chrysostom taught?

What advantage, pray, could be greater than to be seen doing those things which Christ with his own lips declared to be proofs of love to Himself? For addressing the leader of the apostles, He said, "Peter, loves you me?" and when he confessed that he did, the Lord added, "if you love me tend my sheep." The Master asked the disciple if He was loved by him, not in order to get information (how should He who penetrates the hearts of all men?), but in order to teach us how great an interest He takes in the superintendence of these sheep. This being plain, it will likewise be manifest that a great and unspeakable reward will be reserved for him whose labors are concerned with these sheep, upon which Christ places such a high value.

St. Augustine: (354 - 430 A.D.)

Augustine of Hippo also known as **Saint Augustine**, was a theologian and philosopher of Berber origin and the bishop of Hippo Regius in Roman North Africa. His writings influenced the development of Western philosophy and Christianity, and he is viewed as one of the most important Church Fathers of the Latin Church. According to his contemporary, St. Jerome, Augustine "established anew the ancient Faith".

In his youth he was drawn to the Manichaean faith, and later to the Hellenistic philosophy of Neoplatonism. After his conversion to Christianity and baptism in 386, Augustine developed his approach to philosophy and theology, accommodating a variety of methods and perspectives. Believing the grace of Christ was indispensable to human freedom, he helped formulate the doctrine of original sin and made significant contributions to the development of just war theory. When the Western Roman Empire began to disintegrate, Augustine imagined the Church as a spiritual City of God, distinct from the material Earthly City. The segment of the Church that adhered to the concept of the Trinity as defined by the Council of Nicaea and the Council of Constantinople closely identified with Augustine's *On the Trinity*.

Augustine is recognized as a saint and as a preeminent Doctor of the Church. His memorial is celebrated on 28 August, the day of his death. Augustine is the patron saint of brewers, printers, theologians, and many cities and dioceses. His thoughts profoundly influenced the medieval worldview.

Writings:

The Confessions of St. Augustine, City of God, On Christian Doctrine.

How can we apply what St. Augustine taught?

But I do not think that manner which I have said should be adopted in the preaching of predestination ought to be sufficient for him who speaks to the congregation, except he adds this, or something of this kind, saying, "You, therefore, ought also to hope for that perseverance in obedience from the Father of Lights, from whom cometh down every excellent gift and every perfect gift, and to ask for it in your daily prayers; and in doing this ought to trust that you are not aliens from the predestination of His people, because it is He Himself who bestows even the power of doing this. And far be it from you to despair of yourselves, because you are bidden to have your hope in Him, not in yourselves. For cursed is everyone who has hope in man; and it is good rather to trust in the Lord than to trust in man, because blessed are all they that put their trust in Him.

St. Gregory the Great: (540 - 604 A.D.)

Pope Gregory I commonly known as **Saint Gregory the Great**, was the Bishop of Rome from 3 September 590 until his death. He is known for instituting the first recorded large-scale mission from Rome, to convert the then largely pagan Anglo-Saxons. Gregory is also well known for his writings, which were more prolific than those of any of his predecessors as pope. The epithet **Saint Gregory the Dialogist** has been attached to him in Eastern Christianity because of his *Dialogues*.

Gregory was a Roman senator's son and himself the prefect of Rome at 30. Gregory lived in a monastery that he established on his family estate before becoming a papal ambassador and then pope. Although he was the first pope from a monastic background, his prior political experiences may have helped him to be a talented administrator. During his papacy, his administration greatly surpassed that of the emperors in improving the welfare of the people of Rome. Gregory sent missionaries to England, including Augustine of Canterbury and Paulinus of York. Gregory saw the Franks, Lombards, and Visigoths align with Rome in religion. He also combated the Donatist heresy, popular particularly in North Africa at the time.

Throughout the Middle Ages, he was known as "the Father of Christian Worship" because of his exceptional efforts in revising the Roman worship of his day. His contributions to the development of the Divine Liturgy of the Presanctified Gifts, still in use in the Byzantine Rite, were so significant that he is generally recognized as its *de facto* author.

Writings:

The Dialogues of St. Gregory the Great, Pastoral Care.

How can we apply what St. Gregory the Great taught?

There are some also who investigate spiritual precepts with cunning care, but what they penetrate with their understanding they trample on in their lives: all at once they teach the things which not by practice but by study they have learnt; and what in words they preach by their manners they impugn.

St. Anselm: (1033 - 1109 A.D.)

Anselm of Canterbury, also **Anselm of Aosta** after his birthplace and **Anselm of Bec** after his monastery, was an Italian Benedictine monk, abbot, philosopher, and theologian, who held the office of Archbishop of Canterbury from 1093 to 1109. After his death, he was canonized as a saint; his feast day is the 21st of April. He was proclaimed a Doctor of the Church by a papal bull of Pope Clement XI in 1720.

As Archbishop of Canterbury, Anselm defended the church's interests in England amid the Investiture Controversy. For his resistance to the English kings William II and Henry I, he was exiled twice: once from 1097 to 1100 and then from 1105 to 1107. While in exile, he helped guide the Greek Catholic bishops of southern Italy to adopt Roman rites at the Council of Bari. He worked for the primacy of Canterbury over the Archbishop of York and over the bishops of Wales but, though at his death he appeared to have been successful, Pope Paschal II later reversed papal decisions on the matter and restored York's earlier status.

Beginning at Bec, Anselm composed dialogues and treatises with a rational and philosophical approach, which have sometimes caused him to be credited as the founder of Scholasticism. Despite his lack of recognition in this field in his own time, Anselm is now famed as the originator of the ontological argument for the existence of God and of the satisfaction theory of atonement.

Writings:

The Devotions of St. Anselm

What is a key passage in St. Anselm's Devotions?

Say now, O my whole heart, say now to God, I seek Thy face; Thy face, Lord, do I seek. Come now then, O Lord my God, teach Thou my heart when and how I may seek Thee, where and how I may find Thee? O Lord, if Thou art not here, where else shall I seek Thee? But if Thou art everywhere, why do I not behold Thee, since Thou art here present? Surely indeed Thou dwells in the light which no man can approach unto. But where is that light unapproachable? or how may I approach unto it since it is unapproachable? Or who shall lead me and bring me into it that I may see Thee therein? Again, by what tokens shall I know Thee, in what form shall I look for Thee? I have never seen Thee, O Lord my God; I know not Thy form. What shall I do then, O Lord most high, what shall I do, banished as I am so far from Thee?

St. Bernard: (1090 - 1153 A.D.)

Bernard of Clairvaux, venerated as **Saint Bernard** was an abbot, mystic, co-founder of the Knights Templar, and a major leader in the reformation of the Benedictine Order.

Bernard was sent to create the Clairvaux Abbey at an isolated clearing in a glen known as the *Val d'Absinthe*, in Northeastern France. In the year 1128, Bernard attended the Council of Troyes, at which he traced the outlines of the Rule of the Knights Templar, which soon became an ideal of Christian nobility.

In 1130, a schism arose in the church. Bernard was a supporter of Pope Innocent II, arguing against the Antipope Anacletus II.

Bernard advocated crusades in general and convinced many to participate in the unsuccessful Second Crusade, notably through a famous sermon at Vezalay (1146).
Bernard was canonized just 21 years after his death by Pope Alexander III. In 1830 Pope Pius VIII declared him a Doctor of the Church.

Writings:

On Loving God.

How can we apply what St. Bernard taught?

You want me to tell you why God is to be loved and how much. I answer, the reason for loving God is God Himself; and the measure of love due to Him is immeasurable love. Is this plain? Doubtless, to a thoughtful man; but I am debtor to the unwise also. A word to the wise is sufficient; but I must consider simple folk too. Therefore, I set myself joyfully to explain more in detail what is meant above.

We are to love God for Himself, because of a twofold reason; nothing is more reasonable, nothing more profitable. When one asks, Why should I love God? He may mean, What is lovely in God? Or What shall I gain by loving God? In either case, the same sufficient cause of love exists, namely, God Himself.

And first, of His title to our love. Could any title be greater than this, that He gave Himself for us unworthy wretches? And being God, what better gift could He offer than Himself? Hence, if one seeks for God's claim upon our love here is the chiefest: Because He first loved us (I John-4.19).

St. Thomas Aquinas: (1225 - 1274 A.D.)

Thomas Aquinas was an Italian Dominican friar and priest, an influential philosopher and theologian, and a jurist in the tradition of scholasticism from the county Aquino in the Kingdom of Sicily.

Thomas was a prominent proponent of natural theology and the father of a school of thought (encompassing both theology and philosophy) known as Thomism. He argued that God is the source of the light of natural reason and the light of faith. He embraced several ideas put forward by Aristotle and attempted to synthesize Aristotelian philosophy with the principles of Christianity. He has been described as "the most influential thinker of the medieval period" and "the greatest of the medieval philosopher -theologians". According to the English philosopher Anthony Kenny, Thomas was "one of the greatest philosophers of the Western world".

Thomas's best-known works are the unfinished *Summa Theologica*, or *Summa Theologiae* (1265–1274), the *Disputed Questions on Truth* (1256–1259), and the *Summa contra Gentiles* (1259–1265). His commentaries on Christian Scripture and on Aristotle also form an important part of his body of work. He is also notable for his Eucharistic hymns, which form a part of the Church's liturgy.

As a Doctor of the Church, Thomas Aquinas is considered one of the Catholic Church's greatest theologians and philosophers. He is known in Catholic theology as the *Doctor Angelicus* ("Angelic Doctor", with the title "doctor" meaning "teacher"), and the *Doctor Communis* ("Universal Doctor"). In 1999, John Paul II added a new title to these traditional ones: *Doctor Humanitatis* ("Doctor of Humanity/Humaneness").

Other Writings:

Of God and His Creatures

How can we apply what St. Aquinas taught?

Of all human pursuits, the pursuit of wisdom is the more perfect, the more sublime, the more useful, and the more agreeable.

Thomas Aquinas, in his writings, gives detailed images of how angels exist and what types of actions they might take given their stations. For example, Guardian Angels are those angels assigned to humans to help them through their spiritual journey on earth.

On the next page is a map of key locations of the Church Fathers discussed in this book…

CANTERBURY

CLAIRVAUX ABBEY

FONTAINE LES-DIJON

AOSTA

LYON

MILAN

STRINDON

CONSTANTINOPLE

CAESAREA (MAZACA)

NICEA

CARRHAE

ROME

ROCCASECCA

FOSSANOVA

SMYRNA

ANTIOCH

ATHENS

HIPPO

CARTHAGE

THAGASTE

NABLUS

ALEXANDRIA

ST. IGNATIUS - ANTIOCH

CLEMENT OF ROME - ROME

POLYCARP - SMYRNA

JUSTIN MARTYR - NABLUS

ST. IRANAEUS - BORN - SMYRNA, DIED IN LYON

CLEMENT OF ALEXANDRIA - ALEXANDRIA

TERTULLIAN - CARTHAGE

ORIGEN - ALEXANDRIA

ST. CYPRIAN - CARTHAGE

ARCHELAUS - CARRHAE

ST. ATHANASIUS - ALEXANDRIA

ALEXANDER OF ALEXANDRIA - ALEXANDRIA

ST. AMBROSE - MILAN

ST. JOHN CRYSOSTUM - BORN IN ANTIOCH, BISHOP OF CONSTANTINOPLE

ST. AUGUSTINE - THAGASTE AND HIPPO IN TUNISIA

ST. BASIL THE GREAT - CAESAREA (MAZACA)

ST. JEROME - STRINDON, DALMATIA

ST. GREGORY THE GREAT - ROME

ST. ANSELM - BORN AOSTA , DIED - CANTERBURY

ST. BERNARD - BORN - FOUNTAINE LES DIJON, DIED - CLAIRVAUX

ST. THOMAS AQUINAS - BORN ROCCASECCA, DIED - FOSSONAVA

Great Women of the Catholic Church:

And last but certainly not least, we look at some of the great women in the Catholic Church.

St. Mary:

Of course, we must start with the mother of our Lord Jesus, Mother Mary. Not only do we learn a lot about what Mary went through in the Bible, having to submit her life to God by becoming the mother of our savior, but we learn that she is an active mediatrix in our lives today.

Exorcists often mention that it is Mary who drives away demons during an exorcism. Why would horrible demons be afraid of a young woman from Judea? Because Mary submitted herself completely to God and God's light and holiness shines through her. No demon can stand this powerful woman and her reflection of God.

St. Monica: (332 – 387)

Monica was an early North African Christian and the mother of Augustine of Hippo. She is remembered and honored in the Catholic and Orthodox Churches, albeit on different feast days, for her outstanding Christian virtues, particularly the suffering caused by her husband's adultery, and her prayerful life dedicated to the reformation of her son, who wrote extensively of her pious acts and life with her in his *Confessions.* Popular Christian legends recall Monica weeping every night for her son Augustine.

St. Hildegard: (1098 – 1179)

Hildegard of Bingen also known as **Saint Hildegard** and the **Sibyl of the Rhine**, was a German Benedictine abbess and polymath active as a writer, composer, philosopher, mystic, visionary, and medical writer and practitioner. She is one of the best-known composers of sacred monophony, as well as the most recorded in modern history. She has been considered by a number of scholars to be the founder of scientific natural history in Germany.
Hildegard was elected as *magistra* (mother superior) in 1136. She founded the monasteries of Rupertsberg in 1150 and Eibingen in 1165. Hildegard wrote theological, botanical, and medicinal works, as well as letters, hymns, and antiphons for the liturgy. She wrote poems, and supervised miniature illuminations in the Rupertsberg manuscript of her first work, Scivias.

On 7 October 2012, Pope Benedict named her a Doctor of the Church. in recognition of "her holiness of life and the originality of her teaching."

St. Joan of Arc (Jeanne D'Arc): (1412 – 1431)

Joan of Arc is a patron saint of France, honored as a defender of the French nation for her role in the Siege of Orleans and her insistence on the coronation of Charles VII during the Hundred Year's War. Claiming to be acting under divine guidance, she became a military leader who gained recognition as a savior of France.

In 1428, she requested to be taken to Charles, later testifying that she was guided by visions from the archangel Michael, Saint Margaret, and Saint Catherine to help him save France from English domination. Convinced of her devotion and purity, Charles sent Joan, who was about seventeen years old, to the siege of Orléans as part of a relief army. She arrived at the city in April 1429, wielding her banner and bringing hope to the demoralized French army. Nine days after her arrival, the English abandoned the siege. Joan encouraged the French to aggressively pursue the English during the Loire Campaign, which culminated in another decisive victory at Patay, opening the way for the French army to advance on Reims unopposed, where Charles was crowned as the King of France with Joan at his side. These victories boosted French morale, paving the way for their final triumph in the Hundred Years' War several decades later.

She was captured by Burgundian troops on 23 May. After trying unsuccessfully to escape, she was handed to the English in November. She was put on trial by Bishop Pierre Cauchon on accusations of heresy, acting upon demonic visions, and refusing to submit her words and deeds to the judgment of the church. She was declared guilty and burned at the stake on 30 May 1431, aged about nineteen.

In 1456, an inquisitorial court reinvestigated Joan's trial and overturned the verdict. Joan has been revered as a martyr and viewed as an obedient daughter of the Roman Catholic Church and a symbol of freedom and independence. She later became a national symbol of France. In 1920, Joan of Arc was canonized by the Roman Catholic Church and, two years later, was declared one of the patron saints of France.

Kateri Tekakwitha: (1656 – 1680)

Kateri Tekakwitha is a Catholic saint and virgin who was an Algonquin-Mohawk. Born in the Mohawk village, in present-day New York State, she contracted smallpox in an epidemic; her family died and her face was scarred. She converted to Catholicism at age nineteen. She took a vow of perpetual virginity, left her village, and moved for the remaining five years of her life to the Jesuit mission village of Kahnawake. She was beatified in 1980 by Pope John Paul II and canonized by Pope Benedict on 21 October 2012.

Josephine Bakhita: (1869 – 1947)

Josephine Bakhita was a Canossian religious sister who lived in Italy for 45 years, after having been a slave in Sudan. In 2000, she was declared a saint, the first black woman to receive the honor in the modern era.

She was born around 1869 in Darfur (now in western Sudan). She was one of the Daju people, her respected and reasonably prosperous father was the brother of the village chief. She was surrounded by a loving family of three brothers and three sisters; as she says in her autobiography: "I lived a very happy and carefree life, without knowing what suffering was".

In 1877, when she was 7–8 years old, she was seized by Arab slave traders, who had abducted her elder sister two years earlier. She was forced to walk barefoot about 960 kilometers (600 mi) to El-Obeid and was sold and bought twice before she arrived there. Over the course of twelve years (1877–1889) she was sold three more times.

Her fourth owner was a Turkish general, and she had to serve his mother-in-law and his wife, who were cruel to their slaves. Bakhita says: "During all the years I stayed in that house, I do not recall a day that passed without some wound or other. When a wound from the whip began to heal, other blows would pour down on me."

In 1883, Bakhita was bought in Khartoum by the Italian Vice Counsul Callisto Legnani, who did not beat or punish her. Two years later, when Legnani himself had to return to Italy, Bakhita begged to go with him.

On the advice of Legnani's business agent, on 29 November 1888, Michieli left Josephine in the care of the Canossian Sisters in Venice. There, cared for and instructed by the Sisters, Bakhita encountered Christianity for the first time. Grateful to her teachers, she recalled, "Those holy mothers instructed me with heroic patience and introduced me to that God who from childhood I had felt in my heart without knowing who He was."

A young student once asked Bakhita: "What would you do, if you were to meet your captors?" Without hesitation, she replied: "If I were to meet those who kidnapped me, and even those who tortured me, I would kneel and kiss their hands. For, if these things had not happened, I would not have been a Christian and a religious today".

On 1 October 2000, she was canonized as Saint Josephine Bakhita.

Maria Faustyna Kowalska: (1905 – 1938)

Maria Faustyna Kowalska, (born **Helena Kowalska**; also known as **Maria Faustyna Kowalska of the Blessed Sacrament**, was a Polish Catholic religious sister and mystic. Faustyna, popularly spelled "Faustina", had apparitions of Jesus Christ which inspired the Catholic devotion to the Divine Mercy and earned her the title of "Secretary of Divine Mercy".

Throughout her life, Kowalska reported having visions of Jesus and conversations with him, which she noted in her diary. Her biography quoted some of the conversations with Jesus regarding the Divine Mercy devotion.

At the age of 20 years, she joined a convent in Warsaw. She was later transferred to Ptock and then to Vilnius, where she met Father Michal Sopocko, who was to be her confessor and spiritual director, and who supported her devotion to the Divine Mercy. With this priest's help, Kowalska commissioned an artist to paint the first Divine Mercy image, based on her vision of Jesus. Father Sopocko celebrated Mass in the presence of this painting on Low Sunday, also known as the Second Sunday of Easter or (as established by Pope John Paul II), Divine Mercy Sunday.

The Catholic Church canonized Kowalska as a saint on 30 April 2000. She is classified in the liturgy as a virgin and is venerated within the church as the "Apostle of Divine Mercy".

66

We hope you enjoyed this journey through the "Teenager's Guide to the Early Church Fathers." As previously mentioned, we hope to add more and more content to this book so look for these updated versions coming soon.

You can also find many of the great works of the Early Church Fathers at lighthousechristianpublishing.com.

God bless you and we pray that you will be inspired by these great men and women of the church to grow your faith in the Lord Jesus Christ.

Our Father Who Art in Heaven
Hallowed Be Thy Name
Thy Kingdom Come
Thy Will Be Done
On Earth as it is in Heaven
Give us this Day our Daily Bread
And Forgive us our Trespasses,
As We Forgive Those Who Trespass Against Us
A Lead Us not into Temptation
But Deliver Us from Evil
For Thine is the Kingdom, the Power, and the Glory
Forever and Ever
Amen

Hail Mary Full of Grace
The Lord is with Thee
Blessed Art Thou Among Women
And Blessed is the Fruit of Thy Womb, Jesus
Holy Mary, Mother of God
Pray for Us Sinners
Now and at the Hour of Our Death
Amen

www.ingramcontent.com/pod-product-compliance
Lightning Source LLC
Chambersburg PA
CBHW040742110426
42739CB00028B/38

9781643734194